You are loved

AFRICAN ANIMAL SECRETS

FUN FACTS & FASCINATING CREATURES

Alex Birmingham

AFRICAN HOOPOE

Common Name: African Hoopoe

Latin Name: Upupa africana

Habitat: The African Hoopoe is widespread across sub-Saharan Africa. It inhabits a range of environments including open woods, savannas, grasslands, and gardens. They are often seen in areas with trees and shrubs, which provide nesting sites and foraging opportunities.

Size: African Hoopoes are medium-sized birds, typically about 25 to 29 cm (10 to 11.4 inches) in length, with a wingspan of approximately 44 to 48 cm (17.3 to 18.9 inches).

Diet: Their diet mainly consists of insects and other small invertebrates. They are known for foraging on the ground, using their long, curved beaks to probe the soil for food.

Conservation Status: Least Concern. African Hoopoes are common and widespread throughout their range, with no major threats leading to a significant population decline.

African Hoopoes are easily recognizable by their distinctive 'crown' of feathers, which can be raised into a fan. They have a striking appearance with black, white, and cinnamon coloration.

These birds are known for their distinctive "hoop-hoop-hoop" call, which is the origin of their name. They are solitary or found in pairs and are not particularly migratory, although they may move locally in response to changing conditions.

African Hoopoes nest in cavities in trees, cliffs, or walls. Their breeding behavior includes unique rituals such as the male offering food to the female as part of courtship.

The African Hoopoe plays a role in its ecosystem as a predator of insects and other small invertebrates, helping to control their populations. Their presence in diverse habitats and adaptability to different environments make them a common sight in both natural and modified landscapes across Africa.

AFRICAN HOOPOE

AFRICAN GREY PARROT

Common Name: African Grey Parrot

Latin Name: Psittacus erithacus

Habitat: African Grey Parrots are native to the rainforests of West and Central Africa. They prefer dense forests but can also be found in savannas and coastal mangroves.

Size: These parrots are medium-sized, typically around 33 cm (13 inches) in length. They weigh approximately 400 to 500 grams.

Diet: African Grey Parrots are omnivores. Their diet in the wild consists of fruits, nuts, seeds, and berries. They also eat bark and flowers, and occasionally insects and snails.

Conservation Status: Endangered. African Grey Parrots face threats from habitat destruction and the pet trade. Their populations have been declining due to extensive trapping for the bird trade and habitat loss. Conservation efforts are in place to protect these intelligent birds and their habitats.

African Grey Parrots are renowned for their intelligence and ability to mimic human speech, making them one of the most popular avian pets. They have a distinct grey plumage, bright red tails, and sharp, curved beaks. These parrots are known for their problem-solving skills and cognitive abilities that are rare among non-human animals

In the wild, African Grey Parrots are social birds, often found in flocks. They form strong pair bonds and are known for their complex vocalizations and natural mimicry of the sounds in their environment.

The demand for African Grey Parrots in the pet trade has led to significant population declines in some areas. Wild-caught individuals often suffer high mortality rates during capture and transport. International trade in wild-caught African Grey Parrots is restricted under the Convention on International Trade in Endangered Species of Wild Fauna and Flora (CITES).

Conservation efforts are focused on enforcing these trade regulations, protecting habitats, and educating the public about the challenges of keeping these birds as pets and the importance of preserving wild populations.

AFRICAN GREY PARROT

LION

Common Name: Lion

Latin Name: Panthera leo

Habitat: Lions in Africa inhabit a range of environments, including grasslands, savannas, dense scrub, and open woodlands. They are notably found in parts of sub-Saharan Africa, with significant populations in countries like Tanzania, Kenya, South Africa, Botswana, and Namibia.

Size: African lions are among the largest of the big cats. Males typically weigh between 150-250 kg (330-550 lbs) and are about 1.2 meters (4 feet) tall at the shoulder. Females are smaller, usually weighing between 110-180 kg (240-400 lbs).

Diet: Lions are apex predators and primarily carnivorous. They hunt a variety of prey, including wildebeest, zebras, buffaloes, young elephants, rhinos, hippos, and smaller animals like birds and reptiles. They are also known to scavenge when opportunities arise.

Conservation Status: Vulnerable. African lion populations are decreasing. Major threats include habitat loss, human-wildlife conflict, and to a lesser extent, poaching. Their numbers have been reduced significantly in the past few decades, with conservation efforts being put in place to protect these majestic animals and their habitats.

Lions are known for their distinctive manes seen in males, which is a unique feature among big cats. These manes may vary in color and length and can provide an indication of the lion's health and virility.

Socially, lions are unique among big cats as they live in groups called prides. A typical pride consists of several related females, their cubs, and a few males. Females in the pride are often related and stay with the pride for life, whereas males may change.

Lions play a crucial role in their ecosystem as top predators, helping to regulate prey populations and maintain the ecological balance.

Conservation efforts for lions include habitat preservation, reducing human-lion conflicts, and managing areas where they can roam freely. Ecotourism also plays a role in their conservation by providing funds for protection and creating an economic incentive to preserve wildlife.

LION

AFRICAN ELEPHANT

Common Name: African Elephant

Latin Name: There are two species - the African Bush Elephant (Loxodonta africana) and the African Forest Elephant (Loxodonta cyclotis).

Habitat: The African Bush Elephant is primarily found in savannas, grasslands, and woodlands. The African Forest Elephant mainly inhabits the dense rainforests of central and west Africa.

Size: The African Bush Elephant is the larger of the two species and is the largest land animal on Earth. Males can reach 3.2 meters (10.5 feet) at the shoulder and weigh between 4,500-6,800 kg (10,000-15,000 lbs). The Forest Elephant is smaller, with males usually not exceeding 2.5 meters (8.2 feet) in height and a weight of up to 2,700 kg (6,000 lbs).

Diet: African Elephants are herbivores and consume a diet consisting of a wide variety of vegetation including grasses, leaves, bark, and fruit.

Conservation Status: The African Elephant is classified as Vulnerable. However, the African Forest Elephant is critically endangered due to factors such as poaching for ivory and habitat loss. Conservation efforts are in place to protect these species, but they still face significant threats in their natural habitats.

African Elephants are known for their intelligence, strong familial bonds, and complex social structures. They are keystone species, playing a critical role in their ecosystems by shaping habitats, dispersing seeds, and creating water holes used by other animals.

Conservation efforts for African Elephants focus on anti-poaching measures, habitat conservation, and mitigating human-elephant conflicts. International efforts include regulating ivory trade to reduce poaching. Additionally, research and monitoring are vital for understanding elephant behavior and needs, which aids in effective conservation planning.

AFRICAN ELEPHANT

WHITE RHINOCEROS

1.Common Name: White Rhinoceros (or Square-lipped Rhinoceros)

Latin Name: Ceratotherium simum

Habitat: Grasslands and savannas, mainly in South Africa, Namibia, Zimbabwe, and Kenya.
Size: One of the largest rhino species, adult males can weigh up to 2,300 kg (5,070 lbs) and stand about 1.8 meters (6 feet) tall at the shoulder.

Diet: Herbivorous, primarily grazing on grasses.

Conservation Status: Near Threatened, with the Northern White Rhino subspecies considered functionally extinct in the wild.

2.Common Name: Black Rhinoceros

Latin Name: Diceros bicornis

Habitat: Various habitats, including savannas, grasslands, and forests, in eastern and southern Africa.

Size: Smaller than the white rhino, weighing up to 1,400 kg (3,080 lbs) and standing up to 1.6 meters (5.2 feet) tall at the shoulder.

Diet: Herbivorous, primarily browsing on leaves, shoots, and branches of bushes and trees.

Conservation Status: Critically Endangered, mainly due to poaching and habitat loss.

Both species of African rhinoceroses are under severe threat from poaching, driven by the demand for their horns in illegal wildlife trade. Conservation efforts are focused on anti-poaching measures, habitat conservation, and breeding programs.

White rhinoceroses have two horns, are larger and have a square-shaped lip, which is useful for grazing. Black rhinoceroses, although slightly smaller, have a pointed upper lip for browsing foliage. Despite their names, both species are actually gray in color.

These magnificent creatures are known for their impressive size and horns. They play a crucial ecological role in their habitats and are also important for tourism, which in turn supports conservation efforts. Protecting the rhinoceroses is not just about saving a single species but is also crucial for preserving the biodiversity of their ecosystems.

BLACK RHINOCEROS

PLAINS ZEBRA

1. <u>Common Name:</u> Plains Zebra (also known as the Common Zebra)

<u>Latin Name:</u> Equus quagga

<u>Habitat:</u> Grasslands and savannas across Eastern and Southern Africa.

<u>Size:</u> Adults typically weigh between 200-350 kg (440-770 lbs) and stand about 1.3-1.5 meters (4.3-4.9 feet) at the shoulder.

<u>Diet:</u> Herbivorous, primarily grazing on grasses, but also eat leaves and stems.

<u>Conservation Status:</u> Near Threatened, with varying populations depending on the region.

2. <u>Common Name:</u> Mountain Zebra

<u>Latin Name:</u> Equus zebra

<u>Habitat:</u> Mountainous and rocky areas in southwestern Africa.

<u>Size:</u> Slightly smaller than the plains zebra, adults weigh around 240-372 kg (529-820 lbs).

<u>Diet:</u> Herbivorous, feeding on grasses, leaves, twigs, and bark.

<u>Conservation Status:</u> Vulnerable, primarily due to habitat loss and hunting.

Zebras are known for their distinctive black and white stripes, which vary among the species and even among individuals. These stripes are believed to serve several functions, including camouflage, temperature regulation, and social interaction.

Socially, zebras live in groups, and their structure varies by species. Plains and mountain zebras typically form harems with a single stallion and several mares, while Grevy's zebras have more fluid associations.

Conservation efforts for zebras involve habitat protection, anti-poaching measures, and maintaining water sources in arid regions. For Grevy's zebras, specifically, conservation efforts are critical due to their endangered status and are focused on protecting and managing their habitat and water resources.

MOUNTAIN ZEBRA

CHEETAH

Common Name: Cheetah

Latin Name: Acinonyx jubatus

Habitat: Cheetahs are found in various habitats, including dry forests, grasslands, savannahs, and arid environments across several African countries. They require large expanses of land with adequate prey and minimal human disturbance.

Size: Cheetahs are medium-sized big cats. Adults typically weigh between 21 to 72 kg (46 to 159 lbs) and stand about 70 to 90 cm (28 to 35 inches) at the shoulder.

Diet: Cheetahs are carnivores. Their diet primarily consists of small to medium-sized ungulates, including gazelles, impalas, and young wildebeests. They are renowned for their speed, capable of reaching up to 60 to 70 miles per hour in short bursts covering distances up to 1,500 feet, making them the fastest land animals.

Conservation Status: Vulnerable. Cheetah populations have been declining due to habitat loss, human-wildlife conflict, poaching, and declining prey populations. Conservation efforts include habitat restoration, reducing human-wildlife conflict, and breeding programs in wildlife reserves and zoos.

Cheetahs are distinct for their slender, streamlined bodies, long legs, and spotted coat. They have a unique black "tear mark" running from the corner of each eye down the side of the nose to the mouth, which helps to reduce glare from the sun. Unlike other big cats, cheetahs cannot roar but can purr and make other unique vocalizations.

One of the most notable features of cheetahs is their extraordinary acceleration and speed, which they use to chase down prey over short distances. They have several adaptations for speed, including large nasal passages for increased oxygen intake, and a long, flexible spine that allows for large strides.

Cheetahs typically hunt alone or in small family groups, and females are solitary except when raising cubs. Unlike other big cats, male cheetahs can form coalitions, often with their brothers.

Conservation and research efforts focus on understanding cheetah biology, behavior, and ecology, which are crucial for developing effective conservation strategies. Additionally, community involvement in cheetah conservation is key, especially in areas where human activities impact their habitats and prey.

CHEETAH

HIPPO

Common Name: Hippopotamus, often shortened to Hippo

Latin Name: Hippopotamus amphibius

Habitat: Hippopotamuses are found in sub-Saharan Africa. They live in rivers, lakes, and mangrove swamps. Despite being land animals, they spend a considerable amount of time in water, which helps keep their body temperature cool and protects their sensitive skin from the sun.

Size: Hippos are one of the largest land mammals. They can be up to 5 meters (16 feet) in length, stand about 1.5 meters (5 feet) tall at the shoulder, and weigh up to 3,200 kg (7,050 lbs).

Diet: They are primarily herbivores, grazing on grasses and occasionally consuming aquatic plants. A hippo can eat about 35 kg (80 lbs) of grass each night.

Conservation Status: Vulnerable. The hippopotamus population is threatened by habitat loss, illegal hunting (especially for their ivory canines), and conflicts with humans. These threats have caused a decline in their numbers across much of their range. Conservation efforts are focused on habitat protection and reducing human-wildlife conflict.

Hippopotamuses are known for their large, barrel-shaped bodies, enormous mouths and teeth, nearly hairless bodies, and short legs. They have a unique adaptation in their skin which secretes a natural sunscreen substance that is red-colored and is often referred to as "blood sweat."

These animals are social and live in groups called pods, bloats, or herds, typically consisting of 10 to 30 individuals, but sometimes much larger. Groups are led by dominant males, which are territorial in water but not on land.

Hippos are semi-aquatic and spend a large part of the day submerged in water to keep cool under the hot African sun. At night, they venture onto land to graze. Despite their heavy build and short legs, hippos are capable swimmers and can run surprisingly fast over short distances on land.

Their presence in the ecosystem plays a significant role in shaping and maintaining rivers and channels in wetlands. However, their large size and territorial nature can make them a danger to humans, especially when humans encroach on their habitats.

Conservation efforts for hippos include protecting their natural habitats, regulating hunting, and mitigating human-hippo conflicts, especially in areas where their habitats overlap with agricultural lands.

HIPPO

CAPE BUFFALO

Common Name: Cape Buffalo, also known as the Affrican Buffalo

Latin Name: Syncerus caffer

Habitat: Cape Buffaloes are widely distributed in sub-Saharan Africa. They prefer dense forest and savanna habitats but can also be found in floodplains, swamps, and grasslands near water sources. They are dependent on water and seldom found far from drinking sources.

Size: Cape Buffaloes are large and robust animals. They typically weigh between 500 to 1,000 kg (1,100 to 2,200 lbs) and stand around 1 to 1.7 meters (3.3 to 5.6 feet) tall at the shoulder. Males are generally larger and more robust than females.

Diet: They are herbivores and primarily graze on grasses. They also consume leaves and other plant material depending on the availability.

Conservation Status: Least Concern. However, populations are facing threats from habitat loss, diseases (like bovine tuberculosis), and conflicts with humans. Their numbers are stable in well-protected areas but declining in other regions.

Cape Buffaloes are known for their unpredictable nature and can be very dangerous, especially if wounded or threatened. They are a member of the "Big Five" game animals in Africa, a term originally used by hunters to denote the five most difficult animals in Africa to hunt on foot.

These animals are very social and live in large herds, which can consist of several hundred to over a thousand individuals. Herds are matriarchal and consist of females and their offspring, along with subordinate males. Dominant males maintain control over the herd and are responsible for protection and leading to grazing and water sources.

Cape Buffaloes play an important role in their ecosystem by influencing vegetation and serving as prey for large predators like lions and crocodiles. Conservation efforts for Cape Buffaloes focus on habitat protection and managing human-wildlife conflict.

CAPE BUFFALO

AFRICAN PENGUIN

Common Name: African Penguin

Latin Name: Spheniscus demersus

Habitat: African Penguins are native to the southern coast of Africa, particularly found along the coastlines of South Africa and Namibia. They inhabit islands and coastal areas, nesting in colonies on beaches and rocky areas.

Size: African Penguins are relatively small as far as penguins go. They stand about 60-70 cm (24-28 inches) tall and weigh between 2.2 and 3.5 kg (4.9 - 7.7 lbs).

Diet: These penguins primarily feed on fish like anchovies and sardines, supplemented by squid and small crustaceans. Their diet varies depending on the availability of fish and environmental conditions.

Conservation Status: Endangered. The African Penguin population has declined drastically over the past century due to overfishing, which affects their food supply, oil spills, and habitat destruction. Conservation efforts include habitat protection, rehabilitation for oiled penguins, and measures to reduce disturbance and overfishing in key feeding areas.

African Penguins are the only penguin species that breeds in Africa and are known for their distinctive braying sound, which is similar to that of a donkey. They are an important species for biodiversity and are a key attraction for wildlife tourism in South Africa.

AGAMA LIZARD

Common Name: Agama Lizard (specifically referring to the Common Agama, also known as the Red-headed Rock Agama)

Latin Name: Agama agama

Habitat: Agama Lizards are found in a range of habitats across Sub-Saharan Africa. They are commonly seen in areas with rocks and boulders, as well as in urban settings, where they can often be seen basking on walls and rooftops.

Size: The Common Agama can grow to be about 30 cm (12 inches) in length, including its tail.

Diet: These lizards are omnivorous. Their diet typically includes a variety of insects, smaller animals, and vegetation.

Conservation Status: The Common Agama is not currently listed as threatened or endangered. It is a widespread species and is considered to be of Least Concern in terms of conservation status. However, like all wildlife, they can be affected by habitat loss and environmental changes.

Agama Lizards are known for their striking coloration, especially in males, who display vivid colors during the breeding season. The dominant male usually shows a bright red or orange head and a blue body, while females and non-dominant males have more subdued coloration.

AGAMA LIZARD

NILE CROCODILE

Common Name: Nile Crocodile

Latin Name: Crocodylus niloticus

Habitat: The Nile Crocodile is found throughout much of Africa, particularly in the central, eastern, and southern regions of the continent. It inhabits a variety of freshwater environments, including rivers, lakes, marshes, and sometimes in brackish water.

Size: Nile Crocodiles are among the largest crocodile species in the world. They can reach lengths of up to 5 meters (16 feet), although the average size is typically around 4 meters (13 feet). They can weigh as much as 700 kg (1,500 lbs).

Diet: They are opportunistic apex predators and have a varied diet that can include fish, reptiles, birds, and mammals. Large crocodiles are capable of taking down sizeable prey such as zebras, small hippos, and large ungulates.

Conservation Status: Least Concern. The Nile Crocodile is widespread and numerous across much of its range. However, it faces threats from habitat loss and human conflict. In some areas, they are hunted for their skin and meat.

Nile Crocodiles are known for their power and agility both in and out of the water. They play an important role in their ecosystem as predators, helping to maintain the balance of animal populations. Their behavior and biology have also been the subject of interest and study in terms of crocodile conservation and management.

NILE CROCODILE

AFRICAN WILD DOG

Common Name: African Wild Dog

Latin Name: Lycaon pictus

Habitat: African Wild Dogs are found in a variety of habitats ranging from desert areas to dense forests, but they primarily thrive in savannas and arid zones. They are most commonly seen in southern and East Africa, particularly in countries like Botswana, Tanzania, and parts of Zimbabwe and South Africa.

Size: These dogs are medium-sized canines. They typically weigh between 18 to 36 kg (40 to 79 lbs). They stand about 75 cm (30 inches) at the shoulder.

Diet: African Wild Dogs are highly efficient predators and primarily hunt in packs. They feed mostly on antelopes but also hunt for warthogs, rodents, birds, and sometimes large mammals like wildebeests and zebras. Their hunting strategy is based on endurance, chasing their prey over long distances.

Conservation Status: Endangered. Their populations have been declining due to habitat fragmentation, conflict with human activities, disease (like rabies and distemper caught from domestic animals), and competition with larger predators like lions and hyenas.

African Wild Dogs are known for their social structure and cooperative behavior. Packs are usually led by a dominant breeding pair and they are highly social, sharing food and assisting injured or sick members. They have distinctive mottled fur with patches of black, brown, yellow, and white, which varies greatly among individuals, and large rounded ears.

Conservation efforts for African Wild Dogs include habitat restoration, creating wildlife corridors to connect fragmented populations, and vaccination programs to protect them from diseases.

AFRICAN WILD DOG

CHIMPANZEE

Common Name: Chimpanzee

Latin Name: Pan troglodytes

Habitat: Chimpanzees are found in a variety of habitats across Central and West Africa, including tropical rainforests, woodlands, and grasslands near rivers or lakes. They are highly adaptable and can thrive in both primary and secondary forests.

Size: Chimpanzees are relatively large among primates, with adult males typically weighing between 40 and 60 kg (88 to 132 lbs) and standing up to 1.7 meters (5.6 feet) tall when erect. Females are slightly smaller.

Diet: Chimpanzees have an omnivorous diet. They primarily eat fruits, leaves, seeds, tree bark, and plant bulbs. They also hunt and eat insects, eggs, and small animals, including monkeys. Their diet can vary significantly depending on the season and their habitat.

Conservation Status: Endangered. Chimpanzee populations are declining due to habitat destruction, poaching, and the illegal wildlife trade. They are also susceptible to diseases, both natural and those transmitted by humans.

Chimpanzees are our closest living relatives, sharing about 98% of our DNA. They are known for their high intelligence, with the ability to use tools, learn new skills, and exhibit complex social behaviors. They live in social communities typically led by an alpha male and have a complex social structure.

Conservation efforts for chimpanzees include habitat protection, anti-poaching patrols, and public education campaigns to reduce bushmeat trade. Sanctuaries and rehabilitation centers also play a key role in the rescue and rehabilitation of orphaned and injured chimpanzees.

CHIMPANZEE

BABOON

Common Name: Baboon

Latin Name: There are several species, including the Olive Baboon (Papio anubis), Yellow Baboon (Papio cynocephalus), and others within the genus Papio.

Habitat: Baboons are versatile and adapt to a variety of habitats. They are primarily found in savanna and other semi-arid habitats, but can also be found in tropical rainforests and mountains across Africa. They are known for their ability to adapt to human-modified environments as well.

Size: Size varies by species, but adult males typically weigh between 20 to 40 kg (44 to 88 lbs), and can be as heavy as 50 kg (110 lbs) for some species. They stand about 60 to 86 cm (24 to 34 inches) at the shoulder.

Diet: Baboons are omnivorous, their diet includes fruits, grasses, seeds, roots, and bark. They also eat insects and small mammals, and are even known to hunt young antelopes, hares, and birds.

Conservation Status: Most baboon species are not currently endangered, but they do face threats from habitat loss and hunting. They are typically classified as Least Concern, but their populations are affected by expanding human populations and agriculture.

Baboons are known for their high level of social complexity and live in troops that can include dozens to hundreds of members. These troops have a strict social hierarchy, maintained through social grooming and other interactions. Baboons are also notable for their intelligence and have been observed using tools and engaging in tactical behavior when foraging and hunting.

BABOON

SPOTTED HYENA

1. Common Name: Spotted Hyena

Latin Name: Crocuta crocuta

Habitat: Spotted Hyenas are found in a variety of habitats including savannas, grasslands, woodlands, and forests, across sub-Saharan Africa.

Size: They are the largest of the hyena species, with females typically larger than males. Adults can weigh between 40 to 86 kg (88 to 190 lbs) and stand up to 85 cm (33 inches) at the shoulder.

Diet: Highly versatile feeders, spotted hyenas are both predators and scavengers. Their diet mainly consists of carrion, but they are also effective hunters, targeting a variety of animals from small insects to large ungulates.

Conservation Status: Least Concern, but their populations are declining in some areas due to habitat loss and human-wildlife conflict.

2. Common Name: Striped Hyena

Latin Name: Hyaena hyaena

Habitat: Striped Hyenas inhabit savannas, arid regions, and mountainous terrains in North and East Africa, extending into the Middle East and Asia.

Size: Slightly smaller than their spotted cousins, striped hyenas weigh between 26 to 41 kg (57 to 90 lbs) and stand about 70 cm (28 inches) at the shoulder.

Diet: They are primarily scavengers, consuming carrion and leftovers from other predators, but they also eat insects, fruits, and occasionally small animals.

Conservation Status: Near Threatened. Striped hyenas are threatened by habitat destruction, poaching, and persecution by humans.

Hyenas are known for their unique vocalizations, often characterized as 'laughs', which are part of their complex social communication. They live in clans with a social structure that varies by species. Spotted hyenas, in particular, have a matriarchal society, unusual among carnivorous mammals. Hyenas play a crucial role in their ecosystems as scavengers, helping to clean up carcasses and control the spread of diseases.

STRIPED HYENA

WARTHOG

Common Name: Warthog

Latin Name: Phacochoerus africanus

Habitat: Warthogs are widely distributed across sub-Saharan Africa. They are predominantly found in grassland, savanna, and woodland regions. They prefer areas with a good water supply, but are also adaptable to drought conditions.

Size: Warthogs are medium-sized wild pigs. Adult males typically weigh between 60 to 150 kg (130 to 330 lbs) and stand about 63 to 85 cm (25 to 33 inches) at the shoulder. Females are slightly smaller.

Diet: Warthogs are mainly herbivores. Their diet primarily consists of grass, roots, berries, and other plant matter. They are also known to eat insects and occasionally small animals.

Conservation Status: Least Concern. Warthogs are common and widespread across their range. However, they can be susceptible to drought and habitat loss in certain areas.

Warthogs are recognizable by their distinctive facial features, including large curved tusks, which are actually elongated canine teeth, and wart-like growths on their faces. They have a unique habit of kneeling on their front knees while foraging. Warthogs are also known for using burrows created by other animals for shelter and thermoregulation.

These animals live in family groups called sounders, typically consisting of a female and her offspring. Warthogs are not aggressive creatures but can defend themselves fiercely with their tusks if threatened. They play an important role in their ecosystems both as prey for large predators and as grazers.

WARTHOG

MEERKAT

Common Name: Meerkat

Latin Name: Suricata suricatta

Habitat: Meerkats are found in the arid regions of southern Africa, particularly in the Kalahari Desert. They thrive in open country and plains, living in areas with sandy or hard soil which is suitable for digging burrows.

Size: Meerkats are small, standing about 25 to 35 cm (10 to 14 inches) tall when upright. They weigh around 0.5 to 1 kg (1.1 to 2.2 lbs).

Diet: Meerkats are primarily insectivores, meaning their diet consists mainly of insects. They also eat other small animals like lizards, snakes, scorpions, spiders, plants, eggs, and small mammals.

Conservation Status: Least Concern. Meerkats are not currently at risk of extinction; however, like all species, they can be affected by habitat loss and changes in their natural environment.

Meerkats are known for their highly social behavior and live in groups called "mobs" or "gangs" that can consist of up to 50 individuals. A fascinating aspect of meerkat society is their cooperative approach, including taking turns in tasks like looking out for predators while others forage for food.

These small mammals are characterized by their upright stance, often seen standing on their rear legs scanning the horizon for predators. They have a unique adaptation in their eyes that helps protect them from the glare of the sun.

Meerkats have become popular due to their charismatic behavior and social dynamics, often featured in documentaries and as subjects in wildlife studies.

MEERKAT

OSTRICH

Common Name: Ostrich

Latin Name: Struthio camelus

Habitat: Ostriches are native to large parts of Africa, particularly the savannas and Sahel of sub-Saharan Africa. They thrive in open land, including semi-arid and arid regions, where they can find sufficient vegetation.

Size: The Ostrich is the world's largest bird. Adult males can stand up to 2.8 meters (9 feet) tall and weigh as much as 156 kg (345 lbs). Females are somewhat smaller.

Diet: Ostriches are omnivores but primarily feed on plant matter, including seeds, shrubs, grass, and fruits. They also eat insects and other small creatures they find as they forage.

Conservation Status: The common ostrich is listed as Least Concern by the IUCN, but some of its subspecies, particularly the Arabian Ostrich (Struthio camelus syriacus), have become extinct. The primary threats to ostriches include habitat loss and hunting.

Ostriches are flightless but are well adapted for life on the ground. They have long, powerful legs that can cover great distances and are capable of sprinting up to 70 km/h (43 mph), making them the fastest two-legged animal in the world. Ostriches lay the largest eggs of any living land animal.

They have a unique social structure and are often found in small herds that typically contain a dominant male and multiple females. Ostriches are known for their strong legs, which are not only adapted for running but can also be used to deliver powerful kicks as a defense mechanism.

OSTRICH

AFRICAN ROCK PYTHON

Common Name: African Rock Python

Latin Name: Python sebae

Habitat: The African Rock Python is widely distributed in sub-Saharan Africa. It prefers a variety of habitats, including savannas, grasslands, forests, and near water bodies like swamps, lakes, and rivers. It is often found in rocky areas and sometimes close to human habitation.

Size: This species is one of the largest snakes in the world. It can reach lengths of up to 6 meters (20 feet), though the average size is usually around 3 to 4 meters (10 to 13 feet).

Diet: As a constrictor, the African Rock Python preys on a variety of animals. Its diet includes small mammals like rodents, larger mammals such as antelopes, and occasionally birds. It is known for its ability to take down sizable prey, which it suffocates using its powerful coils.

Conservation Status: Not globally threatened but no comprehensive assessment has been done by the IUCN. In some regions, they are at risk due to habitat loss and hunting for their skin and meat.

African Rock Pythons are non-venomous and kill their prey by constriction. They have a striking pattern that helps them blend into their surroundings, providing effective camouflage. This species is known for its strength and has a reputation for being aggressive when threatened. They lay eggs, which the female python incubates and guards until they hatch.

Due to their size and strength, African Rock Pythons are apex predators in their ecosystem, playing an important role in controlling the population of their prey. Their presence is an indicator of a healthy, biodiverse ecosystem.

AFRICAN ROCK PYTHON

WILDEBEEST

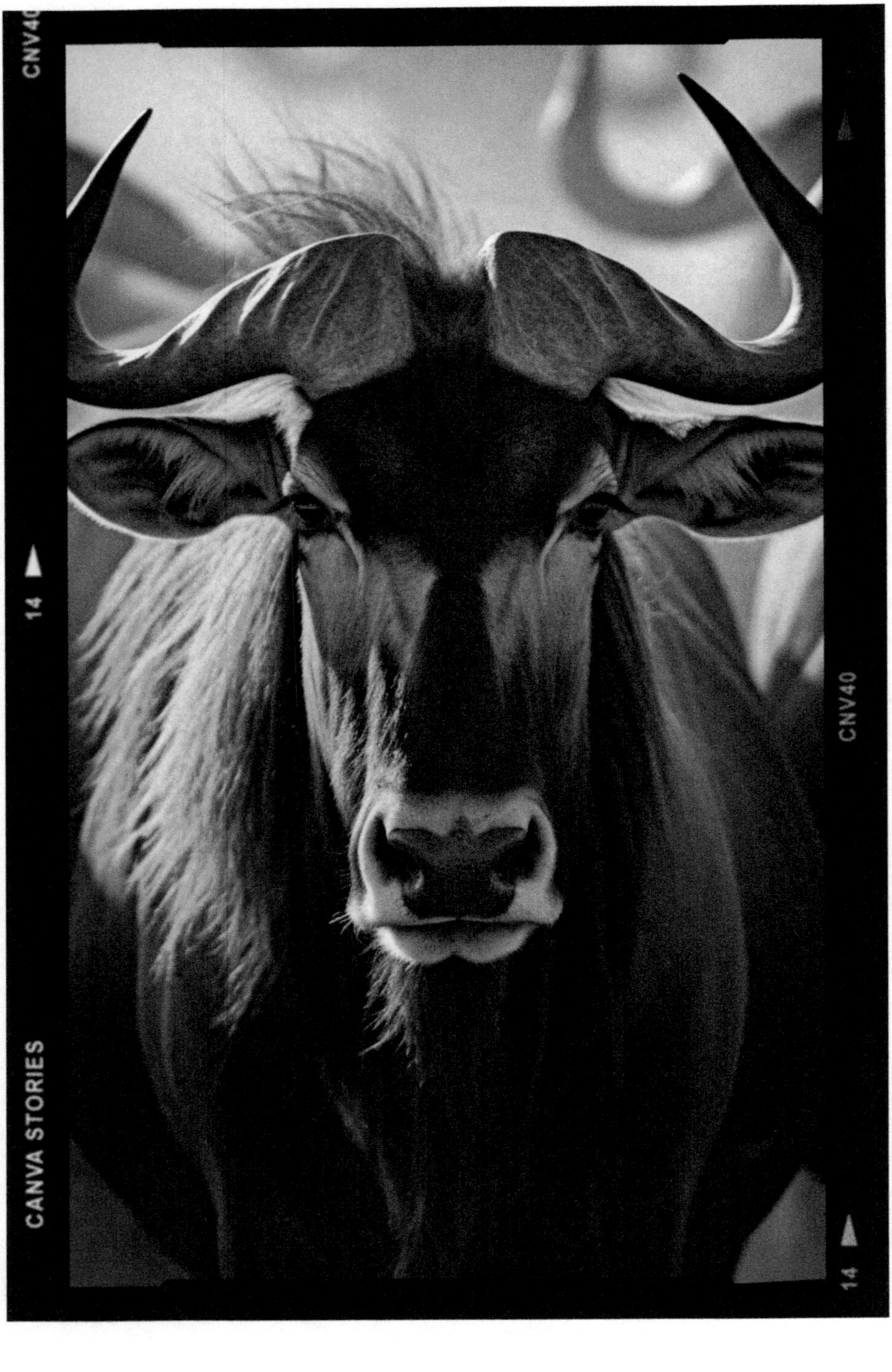

Common Name: Wildebeest

Latin Name: There are two species - the Blue Wildebeest (Connochaetes taurinus) and the Black Wildebeest (Connochaetes gnou).

Habitat: Wildebeests are native to Africa. The Blue Wildebeest is found mainly in the eastern and southern parts of Africa, inhabiting the savannas, grasslands, and open woodlands. The Black Wildebeest is primarily found in the grasslands of southern Africa.

Size: The Blue Wildebeest is larger, with adult males weighing up to 250 kg (550 lbs) and standing about 1.5 meters (4.9 feet) at the shoulder. The Black Wildebeest is smaller, with adult males weighing up to 180 kg (400 lbs).

Diet: Wildebeests are herbivores, primarily grazing on grasses. Their diet varies seasonally according to the availability of different types of grass.

Conservation Status: The Blue Wildebeest is classified as Least Concern, though specific populations may be at risk due to habitat loss and other factors. The Black Wildebeest was once considered endangered due to hunting and loss of habitat but has recovered in recent years thanks to conservation efforts and is now also listed as Least Concern.

Wildebeests are known for their annual migration, especially the spectacular migration of the Blue Wildebeest in the Serengeti-Mara ecosystem. This migration involves over a million individuals and is considered one of the world's most awe-inspiring natural events. They migrate in search of fresh grazing and water, playing a critical role in the biodiversity of the ecosystems through which they travel.

These animals are social and live in large herds. They are a key prey species for large African predators like lions, hyenas, and crocodiles, especially during their migration when they must cross rivers and face these dangerous predators.

WILDEBEEST

OKAPI

Common Name: Okapi

Latin Name: Okapia johnstoni

Habitat: The Okapi is native to the northeastern rainforests of the Democratic Republic of Congo in Central Africa. They primarily inhabit dense, moist, and old-growth forests, often in areas with a dense understory to hide in.

Size: Okapis are medium-sized giraffids. They typically measure about 1.5 meters (4.9 feet) in height at the shoulder and can weigh between 200 and 350 kg (440 to 770 lbs).

Diet: The Okapi is a herbivore. Its diet consists mainly of leaves, buds, shoots, fruits, and fungi. They have a long, flexible tongue, much like their relative, the giraffe, which they use to strip leaves from branches.

Conservation Status: Endangered. The Okapi faces several significant threats, including habitat loss due to logging and human settlement, poaching, and regional conflict. Efforts to protect the Okapi include habitat conservation and anti-poaching measures.

The Okapi is notable for its striking appearance. It has a dark, velvety body, with white-and-black striped legs and hindquarters, which help it blend into the dappled sunlight of its forest habitat. Despite its zebra-like stripes, the Okapi is actually most closely related to the giraffe.

Okapis are solitary animals, coming together only to breed. They are shy and elusive, making them difficult to study in the wild. Their presence is often indicated by their unique footprints or dung rather than direct sightings. The Okapi serves as an important symbol for the biodiversity of the Congo Basin and the need for conservation in this region.

OKAPI

BONOBO

Common Name: Bonobo

Latin Name: Pan paniscus

Habitat: Bonobos are found exclusively in the Democratic Republic of Congo in Central Africa. They inhabit primary and secondary tropical rainforests, particularly in areas along the south bank of the Congo River.

Size: Bonobos are medium-sized primates. Adult bonobos typically weigh between 30 to 60 kg (66 to 132 lbs), with males being slightly larger than females. They stand about 70 to 83 cm (28 to 33 inches) tall when upright on two legs.

Diet: They are omnivorous, with their diet consisting largely of fruits, along with leaves, flowers, bark, seeds, and stems. Bonobos also eat insects, honey, eggs, and small animals including small mammals and reptiles.

Conservation Status: Endangered. The bonobo population is threatened by habitat destruction, particularly from logging and agriculture, as well as by poaching and the bushmeat trade. The ongoing conflict in the region also poses significant challenges to their conservation.

Bonobos share more than 98% of their genetic code with humans, making them, along with chimpanzees, our closest living relatives. They are known for their matriarchal society, where females generally hold higher ranks and lead groups. Bonobos are also noted for their high levels of social and sexual behavior, used as a means for conflict resolution, bonding, and stress reduction.

These primates are highly intelligent, with the ability to show empathy, cooperation, and self-recognition. They are less aggressive than their chimpanzee cousins and are known for their playful and peaceful demeanor.

Conservation efforts for bonobos include habitat protection, law enforcement to prevent poaching and illegal trade, and community-based conservation programs to engage local communities in their protection.

BONOBO

GIRAFFE

Common Name: Giraffe

Latin Name: Giraffa camelopardalis

Habitat: Giraffes are native to various parts of sub-Saharan Africa. They inhabit savannas, grasslands, and open woodlands where they can find their food sources. Their habitat is characterized by open spaces and scattered trees, especially acacia trees which are a primary food source.

Size: Giraffes are the world's tallest mammals. Adult giraffes typically reach heights of 4.3 to 5.7 meters (14 to 19 feet). Adult males can weigh up to 1,930 kg (4,250 lbs), while females are generally lighter, weighing up to 1,180 kg (2,600 lbs).

Diet: Giraffes are herbivores and have a diet that mainly consists of leaves, twigs, and branches of trees, particularly acacia species. Their long necks and tongues (which can be up to 45 cm or 18 inches long) allow them to reach leaves high up in trees that other herbivores can't reach.

Conservation Status: Vulnerable. Giraffe populations are declining due to habitat loss, poaching, and human-wildlife conflict. There are several subspecies of giraffes, some of which are classified as endangered or critically endangered.

Giraffes are known for their long necks and legs, and their unique spotted coat patterns, which vary among the different subspecies. Each giraffe's pattern is unique, much like a human fingerprint.

These animals are social creatures and typically live in groups, although the composition of these groups can be quite fluid. They are non-territorial and roam freely over large areas.

Conservation efforts for giraffes include habitat conservation, anti-poaching patrols, and community-based conservation projects. These efforts aim to protect giraffe populations and their habitats, as well as promote sustainable coexistence with local communities.

GIRAFFE

AFRICAN FISH EAGLE

Common Name: African Fish Eagle

Latin Name: Haliaeetus vocifer

Habitat: The African Fish Eagle is widespread across sub-Saharan Africa. It is commonly found near large bodies of open water, such as lakes, rivers, and coastal areas, where there is an abundant food supply. This bird prefers habitats with large trees for perching and nesting.

Size: The African Fish Eagle is a large bird of prey. It typically measures about 63 to 75 cm (25 to 30 inches) in length, with a wingspan ranging from 2 to 2.4 meters (6.6 to 7.9 feet). Adult females are generally larger than males, weighing up to 3.6 kg (7.9 lbs), while males weigh up to 2.5 kg (5.5 lbs).

Diet: As its name suggests, the diet of the African Fish Eagle is primarily composed of fish. However, it also feeds on birds, carrion, and, less frequently, small mammals. This eagle is known for its skilled fishing technique, where it swoops down over water to catch fish near the surface.

Conservation Status: Least Concern. The African Fish Eagle is widespread and common throughout its range. However, it can be locally affected by environmental pollution, habitat destruction, and changes in fish populations.

The African Fish Eagle is renowned for its distinctive call, which is often considered the sound of Africa. It has a striking appearance, with a white head, chest, and tail, contrasting with a dark brown body and wings. It also has a distinctive black face mask and a bright yellow beak and eyes.

The African Fish Eagle plays an important role in its ecosystem as a top predator. Its presence is indicative of a healthy aquatic ecosystem. These birds are monogamous and known for their elaborate courtship displays. They are also a popular symbol in African culture and appear on the coats of arms of several countries, including Zambia and Zimbabwe.

AFRICAN FISH EAGLE

BLACK MAMBA

Common Name: Black Mamba

Latin Name: Dendroaspis polylepis

Habitat: The Black Mamba is primarily found in the savannas, rocky hills, and open woodlands of sub-Saharan Africa. It is adept at living in both ground-level habitats and arboreal (tree-based) environments.

Size: The Black Mamba is one of the largest venomous snakes in Africa. It can reach lengths of 2 to 3 meters (6.6 to 9.8 feet), with some individuals recorded at over 4 meters (13 feet).

Diet: Its diet mainly consists of small mammals and birds. The Black Mamba uses its speed and potent venom to catch prey, which it then swallows whole.

Conservation Status: The Black Mamba is not currently listed as threatened or endangered. It is widespread and relatively common in its natural habitat, although it faces threats from habitat destruction and is often killed on sight due to its dangerous reputation.

The Black Mamba is renowned for its speed and highly toxic venom, making it one of the most feared snakes in Africa. Despite its name, the snake is not black; its skin color ranges from grey to dark brown. The "black" in its name refers to the color of the inside of its mouth, which is a dark inky black.

This snake is often misunderstood and is not inherently aggressive but will fiercely defend itself if threatened. It is capable of striking at considerable range and may deliver a series of bites in rapid succession. Its venom is neurotoxic, affecting the nervous system and causing symptoms such as difficulty breathing and paralysis.

Because of its potent venom and quick reaction time, the Black Mamba has a fearsome reputation. However, like many snakes, it plays a crucial role in its ecosystem as both predator and prey. Education and awareness are key to reducing conflicts between these snakes and humans.

BLACK MAMBA

ELEPHANT SHREW

Common Name: Elephant Shrew

Latin Name: Macroscelidea (family)

Habitat: Elephant Shrews are found in various habitats across Africa, including forests, savannas, scrublands, and rocky outcrops. Their specific habitat depends on the species, as there are several within the Macroscelidea family.

Size: These small mammals vary in size depending on the species. They typically range from about 10 to 30 cm (4 to 12 inches) in body length, not including the tail. They weigh between 50 to 500 grams (1.8 to 17.6 ounces).

Diet: Elephant Shrews are primarily insectivores. They feed on insects, spiders, small invertebrates, and occasionally seeds and fruits. They have a keen sense of smell and are active foragers.

Conservation Status: The conservation status of Elephant Shrews varies by species. Some are listed as Least Concern, while others are considered Near Threatened or Vulnerable due to habitat loss and fragmentation.

Elephant Shrews are named for their elongated snout, which is somewhat reminiscent of an elephant's trunk. Despite their name and appearance, they are not closely related to shrews but are actually more closely related to a group of African mammals that includes aardvarks, hyraxes, and elephants.

These small mammals are known for their agility and speed. They are able to move quickly to forage for food and evade predators. Most species of Elephant Shrews are monogamous, and pairs maintain and defend their territories.

Elephant Shrews play a role in their ecosystems as both predators of small invertebrates and as prey for larger animals. They are known for their interesting behaviors, including the construction of intricate networks of trails and paths in their habitats.

ELEPHANT SHREW

AFRICAN LUNGFISH

Common Name: African Lungfish

Latin Name: The genus Protopterus includes several species of African Lungfish, such as Protopterus aethiopicus, Protopterus annectens, Protopterus amphibius, and Protopterus dolloi.

Habitat: African Lungfish are found in various parts of Africa, primarily inhabiting freshwater environments like swamps, marshes, and slow-moving rivers. They are well adapted to environments that undergo periodic drying.

Size: The size of African Lungfish varies by species, but they can generally grow quite long. Some species can reach lengths of up to 2 meters (6.6 feet), though most are smaller.

Diet: They have a varied diet that includes fish, amphibians, crustaceans, worms, and plant material. Their feeding habits can change depending on their environment and available food sources.

Conservation Status: The conservation status of African Lungfish varies by species and region. While they are not globally listed as endangered or threatened, habitat destruction and pollution are concerns in some areas.

One of the most fascinating aspects of the African Lungfish is their ability to survive in harsh conditions. During dry periods, when water bodies may dry up, the lungfish can burrow into the mud and form a mucus cocoon around itself, entering a state of estivation (similar to hibernation). In this state, they can survive for months or even years until water becomes available again.

African Lungfish possess both gills and a primitive lung, allowing them to breathe air. This adaptation is particularly useful in oxygen-poor water or when the water dries up. They are considered a living fossil, having changed little in millions of years, and are studied by scientists interested in the evolution of fish to terrestrial vertebrates.

Their ability to breathe air and survive in temporary bodies of water makes them a resilient species, but also means they are susceptible to changes in their environment caused by human activity. Conservation efforts focus on maintaining healthy freshwater ecosystems.

AFRICAN LUNGFISH

GREATER KUDU

Common Name: Greater Kudu

Latin Name: Tragelaphus strepsiceros

Habitat: The Greater Kudu inhabits a range of environments across eastern and southern Africa, including woodlands, bushlands, and dry thornveld. They are known for their adaptability to various habitats but generally prefer areas with dense bush, thickets, or dry riverbeds for concealment.

Size: The Greater Kudu is one of the largest antelopes. Males are significantly larger than females and can stand up to 160 cm (5.2 feet) at the shoulder and weigh between 190 to 270 kg (420 to 600 lbs). Females are smaller, weighing between 120 to 210 kg (260 to 460 lbs).

Diet: Greater Kudus are browsers and feed on a wide variety of leaves, grass, shoots, and occasionally fruits and flowers. They are particularly dependent on water and need to drink regularly.

Conservation Status: The Greater Kudu is classified as Least Concern by the IUCN, though it faces threats from habitat loss and hunting for its meat and impressive horns.

The most distinctive features of the Greater Kudu are its spectacular spiral horns (found only in males) that can grow as long as 72 inches, making them one of the longest horns of any antelope. The body color varies from brownish-grey to reddish-brown, and they have white stripes on their bodies, which help with camouflage.

Greater Kudus are known for their shyness and elusiveness. They are most active in the early morning and late afternoon. Males are typically solitary or form small bachelor groups, while females and young live in small herds.

Due to their size, agility, and ability to jump, Greater Kudus are difficult prey for predators, although they do fall victim to lions, leopards, and African wild dogs. They are also known for their distinctive barking alarm call.

Conservation efforts for Greater Kudus focus on habitat conservation and management, as well as controlled hunting practices in some areas to maintain sustainable populations.

GREATER KUDU

PYGMY FALCON

Common Name: Pygmy Falcon

Latin Name: Polihierax semitorquatus

Habitat: The Pygmy Falcon is native to Eastern and Southern Africa, particularly found in dry bush and thorn scrub regions. Its habitat range includes countries like Kenya, Tanzania, Namibia, and Botswana.

Size: The Pygmy Falcon is one of the smallest raptors on the African continent. It measures about 19 to 20 cm (7.5 to 8 inches) in length and weighs approximately 60 to 80 grams (2.1 to 2.8 ounces).

Diet: Its diet primarily consists of insects, such as termites and ants, but it will also hunt small mammals, birds, and reptiles. Despite its small size, the Pygmy Falcon is an agile and effective predator.

Conservation Status: Least Concern. The Pygmy Falcon is not currently facing any major threats that could significantly impact its population. It is fairly widespread within its habitat range, although its overall population numbers are not well documented.

One interesting aspect of the Pygmy Falcon's behavior is its relationship with weaver birds. In some areas, Pygmy Falcons are known to live in the huge communal nests built by sociable weavers, using empty chambers of the nest as their own.

One interesting aspect of the Pygmy Falcon's behavior is its relationship with weaver birds. In some areas, Pygmy Falcons are known to live in the huge communal nests built by sociable weavers, using empty chambers of the nest as their own.

The Pygmy Falcon is a diurnal bird, meaning it's active during the day. It's known for its striking plumage; males typically have a grey back and head with a white underside, while females have a chestnut back. Both sexes have a distinctive white face with a black eye stripe and collar.

In terms of behavior, Pygmy Falcons are solitary or live in pairs, and they can be territorial. They are often observed perched in high places scouting for prey. Their small size and distinctive call, along with their unique cohabitation with sociable weavers, make them a species of interest in their ecosystem.

PYGMY FALCON

AFRICAN PYGMY HEDGEHOG

Common Name: African Pygmy Hedgehog

Latin Name: Atelerix albiventris

Habitat: In the wild, African Pygmy Hedgehogs are found in a variety of habitats across Central and East Africa, including savannas, grasslands, and agricultural areas. They are adaptable and can thrive in various environments where they can find shelter and food.

Size: African Pygmy Hedgehogs are small mammals. They typically measure about 15 to 25 cm (6 to 10 inches) in length and weigh between 250 to 600 grams (0.5 to 1.3 pounds).

Diet: They are insectivores, primarily feeding on insects. Their diet also includes a variety of other invertebrates like snails and worms, as well as small amounts of fruits and vegetables.

Conservation Status: The wild counterparts of the African Pygmy Hedgehog are not currently listed as endangered or threatened. However, like all wildlife, they are potentially impacted by habitat destruction and changes in their natural environment.

African Pygmy Hedgehogs are known for their distinctive defensive mechanism. When threatened, they roll into a tight ball, with their spines erect to deter predators. These spines are not barbed like those of a porcupine and are relatively harmless to touch when the animal is relaxed.

African Pygmy Hedgehogs are known for their distinctive defensive mechanism. When threatened, they roll into a tight ball, with their spines erect to deter predators. These spines are not barbed like those of a porcupine and are relatively harmless to touch when the animal is relaxed.

These hedgehogs are nocturnal, meaning they are active primarily during the night. In the wild, they spend the day hidden under bushes, rocks, or in burrows to avoid predators and the heat.

While the African Pygmy Hedgehog is popular in the pet trade, it's important to note that caring for one requires specific knowledge of their dietary and environmental needs. They can make interesting pets for those committed to providing proper care, but potential owners should always research and prepare for the responsibilities involved in keeping an exotic animal.

AFRICAN PYGMY HEDGEHOG

NILE SOFT-SHELLED TURTLE

Common Name: Nile Soft-Shelled Turtle

Latin Name: Trionyx triunguis

Habitat: The Nile Soft-Shelled Turtle is found in the freshwater systems of North and East Africa and parts of the Middle East. It inhabits the Nile River and its tributaries, as well as other rivers, lakes, and coastal marshes. This species prefers habitats with soft, muddy bottoms and plenty of aquatic vegetation.

Size: Nile Soft-Shelled Turtles are relatively large. They can reach lengths of up to 1 meter (3.3 feet) and can weigh up to 50 kg (110 lbs), although sizes can vary.

Diet: They are carnivorous and feed primarily on fish, amphibians, and aquatic invertebrates. They are known for their ambush hunting technique, where they bury themselves in the mud and wait for prey to come close.

Conservation Status: The Nile Soft-Shelled Turtle is classified as Vulnerable by the IUCN Red List. It faces threats from habitat loss, pollution, and hunting for consumption and trade.

Nile Soft-Shelled Turtles have a distinctive appearance with a flattened, leathery shell that lacks the hard scutes of most other turtles. Their carapace (upper shell) is olive to dark green in color, and they have long, snorkel-like noses.

These turtles are highly aquatic and are rarely seen far from water. They are known to be very fast in the water and quite agile on land, despite their size. Males are typically smaller and more streamlined than females.

Conservation efforts for the Nile Soft-Shelled Turtle include habitat protection and regulations on hunting and trade. Due to their vulnerable status, efforts are also made to raise awareness about the importance of these turtles in their ecosystems, as they play a crucial role in controlling fish populations and maintaining the health of freshwater habitats.

NILE SOFT-SHELLED TURTLE

AFRICAN GIANT POUCHED RAT

Common Name: African Giant Pouched Rat

Latin Name: Cricetomys gambianus

Habitat: The African Giant Pouched Rat is native to sub-Saharan Africa. It inhabits a variety of environments, including forests, savannas, and densely vegetated areas, often near human settlements.

Size: This species is one of the largest muroid rodents. They typically measure about 25 to 45 cm (9.8 to 17.7 inches) in body length, with a tail almost the same length. Their weight can range from 1 to 1.5 kg (2.2 to 3.3 pounds).

Diet: They are omnivorous, with a diet that includes a variety of plant materials like fruits, seeds, and leaves, as well as insects and other small animals.

Conservation Status: The African Giant Pouched Rat is not currently listed as a species at risk. It is widespread and adaptable, often thriving in areas with human activity.

One of the most distinctive features of the African Giant Pouched Rat is its large cheek pouches, which are similar to those of a hamster. These pouches are used to store and transport food.

These animals are known for their intelligence and strong sense of smell. Remarkably, they have been trained to detect landmines and tuberculosis, making them valuable in certain humanitarian efforts. In landmine detection, their light weight prevents them from triggering explosives, and they are trained to signal to their handlers when they detect the presence of a landmine. For tuberculosis detection, they are trained to recognize the scent of the disease in human sputum samples.

While African Giant Pouched Rats are not commonly kept as pets, their intelligence and trainability have gained them recognition and respect. Conservation and study of this species focus on their ecological impact and their potential utility in tasks like landmine detection and disease screening.

AFRICAN GIANT POUCHED RAT

GREVY'S ZEBRA

Common Name: Grevy's Zebra

Latin Name: Equus grevyi

Habitat: Grevy's Zebras are found in semi-arid grasslands and savannas in Eastern Africa, particularly in Kenya and Ethiopia. They prefer areas with access to permanent water sources but are also adapted to living in extremely arid conditions.

Size: The Grevy's Zebra is the largest of all wild equine species. Adults can stand up to 1.6 meters (5.2 feet) tall at the shoulder and weigh between 350 to 450 kg (770 to 990 lbs).

Diet: They are primarily grazers and feed on a variety of grasses. Their highly adapted digestive systems allow them to subsist on diets of lower nutritional quality than that required by other herbivores in the same areas.

Conservation Status: Endangered. The population of Grevy's Zebras has experienced a significant decline due to habitat loss, competition with livestock for resources, hunting, and drought. Conservation efforts are focused on habitat protection, community-based conservation initiatives, and monitoring of populations.

Grevy's Zebras are characterized by their narrow stripes, which are closer together than those of other zebra species. They have large, rounded ears and a white, stripeless underbelly. Unlike other zebra species, their social structure is more fluid, often forming loose associations rather than permanent herds.

Another distinctive feature of Grevy's Zebras is their highly adapted survival skills in arid environments. They can survive for up to five days without water, although they will drink daily when water is available. Foals can walk just minutes after birth, an important adaptation for survival in areas with predators.

Conservation of Grevy's Zebras involves not just protection of the animals but also sustainable management of water resources and grasslands to ensure their long-term survival. They are an important species for the biodiversity of the ecosystems in which they live, and their conservation is crucial for maintaining the ecological balance.

GREVY'S ZEBRA

AARDWOLF

Common Name: Aardwolf

Latin Name: Proteles cristata

Habitat: The Aardwolf is found in two main regions in Africa: Eastern and Southern Africa. It prefers open, dry plains and bushland, avoiding mountainous areas. Aardwolves are typically found in areas with an abundance of termites, which are their primary food source.

Size: Aardwolves are relatively small and slender hyenas. They typically measure about 55 to 80 cm (22 to 31 inches) in length, with a tail of 20 to 30 cm (8 to 12 inches), and stand about 40 to 50 cm (16 to 20 inches) at the shoulder. They weigh between 8 to 14 kg (18 to 31 lbs).

Diet: Unlike other hyena species, Aardwolves are insectivorous, specializing in termites, particularly those of the genus Trinervitermes. They have adapted to this diet with strong, sticky tongues which they use to lick up large numbers of termites.

Conservation Status: Least Concern. The Aardwolf is not currently considered endangered or threatened. However, they are susceptible to habitat loss and occasionally to poisoning, often indirectly through pesticides used to control locusts and other pests.

Aardwolves have a distinct appearance with a yellowish-brown coat and several vertical black stripes and a bushy tail. They have a mane of long hair along the back, which stands erect when the animal is threatened to make it appear larger.

Aardwolves are nocturnal, spending the day in burrows, and are rarely seen. They are generally solitary or live in monogamous pairs. Communication between aardwolves involves a variety of vocalizations, as well as scent marking with their anal glands.

Despite their name and hyena-like appearance, aardwolves do not hunt large prey and are not scavengers. Their role in controlling termite populations is beneficial for their ecosystem. Conservation efforts for aardwolves focus on habitat preservation and minimizing the impact of pesticides on their food sources.

AARDWOLF

RED LIONFISH

Common Name: Lionfish (Red Lionfish and Devil Firefish are common types)

Latin Name: The genus Pterois, particularly Pterois volitans (Red Lionfish) and Pterois miles (Devil Firefish)

Habitat: Lionfish are native to the Indo-Pacific region, including the South Pacific, the Indian Ocean, and the Red Sea. They inhabit coral reefs, lagoons, and rocky crevices. Notably, they have become an invasive species in the Atlantic Ocean, including the Caribbean and the Southeastern United States.

Size: Lionfish can grow to about 30 to 35 cm (12 to 14 inches) in length.

Diet: They are carnivorous and primarily feed on small fish and crustaceans. Lionfish are skilled hunters, using their fan-like fins to corner prey before swallowing them whole.

Conservation Status: Not considered endangered in their native habitat. However, as an invasive species in the Atlantic, they pose a significant threat to local ecosystems due to their predatory nature and lack of natural enemies.

Lionfish are known for their striking appearance, characterized by bold red, white, and black stripes, and an array of venomous spines. These spines are used primarily for defense and can deliver a painful sting to humans.

In their native habitats, lionfish play a role in the balance of marine ecosystems. However, in the Atlantic and Caribbean, they have become a major ecological problem, preying on native fish and competing for food resources. Efforts to control their population in these areas include organized culls and encouraging their consumption as a food source, as lionfish meat is considered a delicacy.

It's important to note that the term "African Lionfish" is not commonly used in scientific or conservation contexts, and typically, references to "lionfish" are regarding the species from the Indo-Pacific that have become invasive in the Atlantic.

DEVIL FIREFISH

MANDRILL

Common Name: Mandrill

Latin Name: Mandrillus sphinx

Habitat: Mandrills primarily reside in the tropical rainforests of western Central Africa, particularly in countries like Gabon, Cameroon, Congo, and Equatorial Guinea. They prefer dense forests and avoid open areas, living in regions with abundant food and water resources.

Size: Mandrills are the largest of all monkeys. Males are significantly larger than females. An adult male typically weighs between 19 to 37 kg (42 to 82 lbs) but can weigh as much as 54 kg (119 lbs), and stands about 60 cm (2 feet) tall. Females are about half the size of males.

Diet: Mandrills are omnivorous. Their diet consists of fruits, seeds, leaves, stems, insects, fungi, and occasionally small vertebrates.

Conservation Status: Vulnerable. The primary threats to Mandrills include habitat destruction due to logging and agricultural expansion, as well as hunting for bushmeat.

Mandrills are known for their striking coloration and prominent facial features. Adult males have bright blue and red skin on their faces and buttocks. They have a distinctive red and blue snout, and their coloration becomes more vibrant as they mature and during breeding seasons. Females and young mandrills have duller coloration.

These primates live in large social groups, often consisting of hundreds of individuals, making them one of the most socially complex of all monkey species. The social structure within a mandrill troop is primarily organized around maternal lineage.

Mandrills are primarily terrestrial, spending a significant amount of time on the ground in the dense forest underbrush, although they can climb trees and are adept at foraging in different levels of the forest canopy.

Conservation efforts for Mandrills include habitat protection and anti-poaching measures. They are also present in several protected areas across their range, which helps to safeguard their populations. Additionally, education and awareness programs are important for reducing hunting pressures.

MANDRILL

SERVAL

Common Name: Serval

Latin Name: Leptailurus serval

Habitat: Servals are found in various habitats across sub-Saharan Africa. They prefer areas with tall grasses and proximity to water bodies, such as reed beds and wetlands. Their range includes savannas, mountainous areas at certain altitudes, and areas adjacent to forests.

Size: Servals are medium-sized wild cats. They typically weigh between 9 to 18 kg (20 to 40 lbs), with males being larger than females. They stand about 54 to 62 cm (21 to 24 inches) at the shoulder. One of their distinctive features is their long legs relative to body size.

Diet: Servals are carnivorous, primarily hunting small animals such as rodents, birds, frogs, insects, and fish. They are skilled hunters, known for their ability to leap high into the air to catch birds or to pounce on prey after locating it with their acute hearing.

Conservation Status: Least Concern. While servals are widespread and not currently considered endangered, they face threats from habitat loss and hunting. In some areas, they are hunted for their pelts, and in others, they are killed by farmers protecting livestock.

Servals have a distinctive appearance, with golden-yellow to buff-colored fur and black spots and stripes. They have large ears and a small head, which aid in their hunting abilities.

These cats are solitary and territorial animals. They use scent marking to communicate and establish territories. Servals are also known for their ability to climb and swim, although they primarily hunt on the ground.

In terms of behavior, servals are mostly nocturnal but may also be active during the day, especially in cooler weather. They are elusive and are not often seen by humans in the wild.

Conservation efforts for servals include habitat protection and legal protections against hunting and trade. As with many wild cat species, understanding their ecological role and raising awareness about their conservation needs are key components of efforts to ensure their long-term survival.

SERVAL

FENNEC FOX

Common Name: Fennec Fox

Latin Name: Vulpes zerda

Habitat: The Fennec Fox is native to the Sahara Desert and other arid regions in North Africa. It is well-adapted to life in harsh desert environments, inhabiting areas with sandy soils and sparse vegetation.

Size: The Fennec Fox is the smallest of the fox species. It typically weighs about 0.7 to 1.6 kg (1.5 to 3.5 lbs) and has a body length of approximately 24 to 41 cm (9 to 16 inches), not including a 20 to 30 cm (8 to 12 inch) tail.

Diet: They are omnivorous, with a diet that includes insects, small rodents, birds, eggs, and various types of plants and fruits. Their diet is supplemented by the dew they collect from their dens and the moisture found in food.

Conservation Status: Least Concern. While Fennec Foxes are not currently at risk of extinction, they face threats from habitat loss, the fur trade, and capture for the exotic pet trade.

One of the most distinctive features of the Fennec Fox is its large ears, which can be as long as 15 cm (6 inches). These ears help dissipate heat and enhance their hearing, allowing them to detect prey and predators at a distance. They have a cream-colored coat that helps reflect heat and provides camouflage in the desert environment.

Fennec Foxes are nocturnal, which helps them avoid the extreme heat of the desert day. They live in burrows that they dig in the sand, which provide shelter from the heat and protection from predators.

Socially, Fennec Foxes are known to be more social than other fox species. They live in small communities, often consisting of a mated pair and their offspring. Communication among Fennec Foxes involves a variety of vocalizations, purrs, and whimpers.

Their adaptations to desert life, including a highly efficient kidney that helps limit water loss, make them a remarkable example of evolutionary adaptation. Conservation efforts for Fennec Foxes focus on habitat preservation and regulations against illegal trade.

FENNEC FOX

AFRICAN HORNBILL

Common Name: African Hornbills

Latin Name: The family Bucerotidae includes various species, such as the Southern Ground Hornbill (Bucorvus leadbeateri), the African Grey Hornbill (Tockus nasutus), and the Red-billed Hornbill (Tockus erythrorhynchus), among others.

Habitat: African Hornbills are found across sub-Saharan Africa in a variety of habitats, including savannas, woodlands, and tropical forests. Each species has its preferred habitat, with some favoring open grasslands and others dwelling in dense forests.

Size: The size of African Hornbills varies significantly among species. The smaller hornbills, like the Red-billed Hornbill, can be around 35 cm (14 inches) in length, while the larger species, such as the Southern Ground Hornbill, can reach up to 130 cm (51 inches) in length and weigh about 4 kg (8.8 lbs).

Diet: Most hornbills are omnivorous, feeding on fruits, insects, small animals, and birds. The diet can vary greatly depending on the species and the habitat in which they live.

Conservation Status: The conservation status of African Hornbills varies by species. While some are common and widespread, others are facing threats from habitat loss and hunting. The Southern Ground Hornbill, for example, is classified as Vulnerable due to habitat destruction and decline in population.

African Hornbills are known for their long, down-curved bills and a casque (a hollow structure) on top of the bill in some species. They are characterized by their unique breeding behavior, where the female seals herself inside a tree cavity or a rock crevice with a mud wall during the nesting period, leaving only a small slit through which the male feeds her and the chicks.

Hornbills play a significant role in their ecosystems as seed dispersers and as predators of insects and small animals. Their presence is indicative of the health of the environment.

Conservation efforts for African Hornbills include habitat protection and restoration, as well as research and monitoring programs to better understand their ecological needs and population dynamics. In some areas, conservation initiatives also involve local communities in the protection of these birds and their habitats.

AFRICAN HORNBILL

AARDVARK

Common Name: Aardvark

Latin Name: Orycteropus afer

Habitat: The Aardvark is widely distributed across sub-Saharan Africa, inhabiting a range of environments including savannas, grasslands, woodlands, and bushland. They prefer areas that have sufficient cover and sandy or soft soils suitable for digging.

Size: Aardvarks are medium-sized mammals. They typically weigh between 40 to 65 kg (88 to 143 lbs) and measure about 1 to 1.3 meters (3.3 to 4.3 feet) in length, excluding the tail, which can add an additional 60 to 70 cm (24 to 28 inches).

Diet: Aardvarks are specialized in feeding primarily on ants and termites. They use their strong claws to dig into ant hills or termite mounds and then capture their prey using their long, sticky tongue. They can consume thousands of insects in a single night.

Conservation Status: Least Concern. While aardvarks are widespread and not currently at risk of extinction, they are affected by habitat destruction and hunting in some areas. Their secretive and nocturnal nature makes it challenging to determine precise population numbers.

Aardvarks are unique in appearance, with a pig-like snout used for sniffing out food, large, powerful digging claws, and long, rabbit-like ears. They have a stout body and a distinctive arched back.

These animals are primarily nocturnal and solitary, spending the day in burrows that they excavate themselves. These burrows can be extensive, with long tunnels and multiple entrances, and are often used by other animals as well.

Aardvarks have a significant ecological role, particularly in controlling termite and ant populations. Their digging activities also contribute to soil aeration and the creation of habitats for other species.

Conservation efforts for aardvarks include habitat preservation and research to better understand their ecological impact and behavior. They are often elusive and not well understood, which makes scientific study crucial for their conservation.

AARDVARK

AFRICAN SPOONBILL

Common Name: African Spoonbill

Latin Name: Platalea alba

Habitat: African Spoonbills are found in various parts of Africa, predominantly in regions south of the Sahara. They inhabit shallow freshwater wetlands, rivers, lakes, and marshes. They prefer areas with standing water and muddy margins, which are ideal for their feeding habits.

Size: African Spoonbills typically measure about 90 cm (35 inches) in length. They have a wingspan of approximately 120 to 135 cm (47 to 53 inches) and weigh around 1.2 to 2.1 kg (2.6 to 4.6 lbs).

Diet: Their diet primarily consists of fish, aquatic invertebrates, small amphibians, and crustaceans. They feed by wading through shallow water and sweeping their distinctive spoon-shaped bill back and forth to catch prey.

Conservation Status: Least Concern. The African Spoonbill is generally widespread and common throughout its range, but like many waterbirds, it can be affected by changes in water quality and habitat loss due to the draining of wetlands, pollution, and human disturbances.

The African Spoonbill is easily recognizable by its long legs, white plumage, and long, flat, spoon-shaped bill. They lack the crest of feathers that some other spoonbill species have. During the breeding season, they develop a reddish patch on their breasts and a yellowish patch at the base of the bill.

These birds are social and often seen in groups, especially when feeding and roosting. They are known to breed in colonies, sometimes with other waterbird species. Nests are usually built in trees, reeds, or shrubs near water.

The African Spoonbill is not typically a migratory bird but may move locally depending on water levels and food availability. Their breeding and feeding behaviors, as well as their reliance on wetland habitats, make them important indicators of the health of their aquatic ecosystems.

Conservation efforts for the African Spoonbill include wetland conservation and management, pollution control, and monitoring populations to detect any significant changes that might indicate environmental problems.

AFRICAN SPOONBILL

VERVET MONKEY

Common Name: Vervet Monkey

Latin Name: Chlorocebus pygerythrus

Habitat: Vervet Monkeys are widely distributed across sub-Saharan Africa. They are adaptable animals and inhabit a variety of environments including savannas, woodlands, coastal forests, and riverine areas. They can also be found living in proximity to human settlements.

Size: Vervet Monkeys are medium-sized primates. They typically weigh between 3.5 to 8 kg (7.7 to 17.6 lbs), with males generally being larger than females. They have a body length ranging from 40 to 60 cm (16 to 24 inches), with a tail almost as long as the body.

Diet: They are omnivorous and have a varied diet that includes fruits, leaves, seeds, flowers, and insects. They also adapt to consume other food items available in their habitats, including crops and human food waste in areas near settlements.

Conservation Status: Least Concern. Vervet Monkeys are common and widespread across their range. However, they face threats from habitat loss, hunting for bushmeat, and conflict with humans, particularly in areas where they raid crops.

Vervet Monkeys are known for their distinctive grey body fur and black faces surrounded by a white fringe. They have long, agile limbs and a tail used for balance.

These monkeys live in highly social groups called troops, which can consist of several dozen individuals. Social interactions within troops are complex, involving grooming, vocal communications, and various hierarchical behaviors.

Vervet Monkeys play a significant role in their ecosystems, particularly as seed dispersers due to their fruit-based diet. They are also important for studying social behavior and communication in primates.

In terms of conservation and management, efforts typically focus on habitat conservation and mitigating human-wildlife conflict, especially in areas where vervet monkeys are seen as agricultural pests. Education and awareness programs can also help in promoting coexistence between vervet monkeys and local communities.

VERVET MONKEY

SECRETARY BIRD

Common Name: Secretary Bird

Latin Name: Sagittarius serpentarius

Habitat: The Secretary Bird is native to sub-Saharan Africa and is typically found in open grasslands and savannas. It prefers open, flat terrain where it can easily spot and pursue prey. Unlike many other bird species of prey, Secretary Birds are largely terrestrial, spending most of their time on the ground.

Size: Secretary Birds are large birds of prey, standing about 1.3 meters (4 feet) tall. They have a wingspan of about 2.1 meters (7 feet) and weigh around 2.3 to 4.6 kg (5 to 10 lbs).

Diet: Their diet primarily consists of insects, small mammals, and reptiles, especially snakes. Secretary Birds are renowned for their ability to kill snakes, including venomous species. They use their long legs to stomp on their prey or to flush it out of tall grasses.

Conservation Status: Vulnerable. The Secretary Bird is facing threats from habitat loss due to agricultural expansion, as well as from changes in land use that reduce the availability of their prey. Additionally, they are sometimes persecuted due to perceived threats to poultry, although such incidents are rare.

The Secretary Bird is easily recognized by its long legs, eagle-like body, and distinctive quill-like feathers at the back of its head, which resemble office pens traditionally tucked behind a person's ear, leading to its unique name. It has a predominantly grey and white body with black wing tips and tail feathers.

These birds are solitary or occur in pairs, often seen walking through grasslands searching for food. They are also capable fliers, though they spend most of their time on the ground.

The Secretary Bird plays a crucial role in controlling populations of agricultural pests and venomous snakes. Conservation efforts for these birds include habitat protection and public education to highlight their importance as natural pest controllers and their unique role in the ecosystem.

SECRETARY BIRD

AFRICAN CIVET

Common Name: African Civet

Latin Name: Civettictis civetta

Habitat: The African Civet is widely distributed across sub-Saharan Africa. It inhabits a variety of environments, including forests, savannas, and bushlands. African Civets are adaptable and can live in both primary and secondary habitats, often near water sources.

Size: The African Civet is one of the largest civet species. It typically weighs between 7 to 20 kg (15 to 44 lbs) and measures about 70 to 95 cm (28 to 37 inches) in length, not including the tail, which can add an additional 30 to 47 cm (12 to 19 inches).

Diet: African Civets are omnivorous. Their diet includes small mammals, insects, birds, eggs, fruit, and vegetation. They are opportunistic feeders and will also scavenge.

Conservation Status: Least Concern. The African Civet is widespread and relatively common in its range. However, it faces threats from habitat destruction and fragmentation, and in some areas, it is hunted for its fur and for civetone, a musky compound collected from its perineal glands and used in perfumery.

African Civets are distinctive for their black and white patterning, though the pattern can vary greatly between individuals. They have a stocky build with short legs, a long body, and a small head with a pointed snout.

These animals are nocturnal and solitary, spending the day sleeping in dense vegetation or burrows. They are known for their secretive nature and are seldom seen by humans.

The African Civet plays a role in the ecosystem as both a predator and a seed disperser, due to its varied diet. Its omnivorous feeding habits and adaptability to different environments make it an important part of the ecological balance in its habitats.

Conservation efforts for the African Civet include habitat preservation and controlling hunting and trade where it occurs. Due to their elusive nature, more research is often needed to fully understand their population dynamics and conservation needs.

AFRICAN CIVET

NILE MONITOR LIZARD

Common Name: Nile Monitor Lizard

Latin Name: Varanus niloticus

Habitat: The Nile Monitor Lizard is found throughout much of Africa, particularly along the Nile River. It inhabits a range of environments, including savannas, forests, and swamps, but is always found near water sources like rivers, lakes, and wetlands.

Size: Nile Monitor Lizards are among the largest lizards in Africa. They can reach lengths of about 1.5 to 2 meters (4.9 to 6.6 feet), with some individuals growing even larger.

Diet: They are opportunistic carnivores and scavengers. Their diet includes a wide variety of food items such as fish, birds, small mammals, insects, amphibians, crocodile eggs, and other reptile eggs. They are also known to scavenge carrion.

Conservation Status: Least Concern. Nile Monitor Lizards are widespread and adaptable, making them not currently at risk of significant population decline. However, they can be locally affected by habitat loss and hunting.

Nile Monitor Lizards are distinguished by their strong, muscular bodies, long necks, and powerful tails. They have a distinct pattern of light and dark bands on their bodies and tails. They are excellent swimmers and climbers, allowing them to access a variety of prey and environments.

These lizards are solitary and territorial. They are known for their intelligence and have been observed using tools and displaying problem-solving skills, particularly in captivity.

Nile Monitor Lizards play an important role in their ecosystems as both predators and scavengers, helping to control populations of other animals and clean up carrion. They are also culturally significant in some African societies but are often feared due to their size and aggressive nature when threatened.

Conservation efforts for Nile Monitor Lizards generally focus on habitat preservation and education to reduce human-wildlife conflict. In some areas, they are hunted for their meat and skin, which needs to be managed to ensure sustainable populations.

NILE MONITOR LIZARD

AFRICAN GROUND SQUIRREL

Common Name: African Ground Squirrel

Latin Name: The genus Xerus, which includes several species such as the Cape Ground Squirrel (Xerus inauris) and the Unstriped Ground Squirrel (Xerus rutilus).

Habitat: African Ground Squirrels are found throughout much of Africa, particularly in savannas, grasslands, and arid regions. They favor environments with soft soil that allows for easy burrowing.

Size: The size of African Ground Squirrels varies among species. They typically range from about 35 to 45 cm (14 to 18 inches) in body length, with a similar length tail.

Diet: They are primarily herbivorous, feeding on roots, bulbs, fruits, and seeds. They may also consume insects. Their diet can vary based on seasonal availability of food.

Conservation Status: Most species of African Ground Squirrels are not currently considered endangered. They are widespread and adaptable to various environments. However, like many species, they can be impacted by habitat loss and changes in land use.

African Ground Squirrels are notable for their long bushy tails and the social behavior they exhibit. Some species, like the Cape Ground Squirrel, have distinctive stripes on their backs, while others do not.

These ground squirrels live in burrows which they dig themselves. They are social animals, often forming colonies with complex social structures. They use their tails as a shield against the sun—holding them over their bodies for shade.

African Ground Squirrels are diurnal, meaning they are active during the day. They spend a significant amount of time foraging for food and can often be seen standing upright on their hind legs, scanning their surroundings for predators.

Conservation efforts for these squirrels generally involve preserving their natural habitats and ensuring sustainable land use practices. Their role in the ecosystem includes seed dispersal, which contributes to the health of their habitats, and serving as prey for various predators.

AFRICAN GROUND SQUIRREL

BONGO

Common Name: Bongo

Latin Name: Tragelaphus eurycerus

Habitat: Bongos are native to Africa and are found primarily in rainforests with dense undergrowth, across Central, West, and East Africa. They prefer habitats with plenty of cover for concealment.

Size: Bongos are among the largest of the African forest antelope species. An adult bongo can weigh between 200 to 405 kg (440 to 892 lbs) and stand about 1.1 to 1.3 meters (3.6 to 4.3 feet) tall at the shoulder.

Diet: They are herbivores and primarily feed on leaves, buds, shoots, roots, and fruits. Bongos are also known to consume charcoal from burned trees, possibly to aid in digestion or as a mineral supplement.

Conservation Status: The Eastern Bongo is classified as Critically Endangered, while the Western Bongo is classified as Near Threatened. They face threats from habitat loss due to logging and agriculture, as well as from poaching for their meat and horns.

Bongos are notable for their striking appearance, with a bright reddish-brown coat, black and white markings, long slightly spiraled horns (in both sexes), and white stripes running down their sides. This coloration provides excellent camouflage in their forest habitats.

These antelopes are mostly nocturnal and elusive, making them difficult to observe in the wild. They are generally shy, solitary or found in small groups, and are known for their keen sense of hearing and smell.

Conservation efforts for the bongo include habitat preservation, anti-poaching measures, and breeding programs in zoos and wildlife reserves. Reintroduction programs, particularly for the Eastern Bongo in Kenya, are also underway to help restore wild populations.

BONGO

GORILLA

Common Name: Gorilla

Latin Name: The genus Gorilla is divided into two species: Eastern Gorillas (Gorilla beringei) include the Mountain Gorilla (Gorilla beringei beringei) and the Eastern Lowland Gorilla (Gorilla beringei graueri). Western Gorillas (Gorilla gorill) include the Western Lowland Gorilla (Gorilla gorilla gorilla) and the Cross River Gorilla (Gorilla gorilla diehli).

Habitat: Gorillas primarily inhabit the tropical rainforests of central Africa. Mountain Gorillas are found in higher altitude montane and bamboo forests, while Lowland Gorillas inhabit lowland tropical forests.

Size: Gorillas are the world's largest primates. Adult male gorillas, known as 'silverbacks' due to the silver saddle of hair on their backs, can weigh between 136 to 195 kg (300 to 430 lbs) and stand up to 1.7 meters (5.6 feet) in height when upright. Females are smaller, typically weighing half as much as males.

Diet: Gorillas are predominantly herbivorous. Their diet consists mainly of leaves, stems, bamboo shoots, and fruits. They also eat small insects, like termites and ants.

Conservation Status: All gorilla species and subspecies are listed as Critically Endangered or Endangered. They face numerous threats, including habitat destruction due to logging and agricultural expansion, poaching, disease (notably Ebola), and the impacts of civil unrest in some regions.

Gorillas have a complex social structure and live in groups typically led by one dominant male. They are known for their strong family bonds and intelligent behavior, including the use of tools and complex communication.

Gorillas share about 98% of their DNA with humans, making them one of our closest relatives in the animal kingdom. They play a crucial role in their ecosystem by aiding seed dispersal and maintaining forest diversity.

Conservation efforts for gorillas include habitat preservation, anti-poaching measures, and disease control. Ecotourism, when conducted responsibly, also plays a role in gorilla conservation by providing funding and creating local economic incentives for protection. International collaboration and support are essential for the conservation of these magnificent animals and their habitat.

GORILLA

AFRICAN ANIMAL SECRETS

FUN FACTS & FASCINATING CREATURES

Alex Birmingham

More Alex Birmingham Books

Follow me on Amazon by scanning this QR code or go to this URL: https://www.amazon.com/Alex-Birmingham/e/B0B7GZQRLC

Subscribe to my newsletter on https://alexbirmingham.substack.com

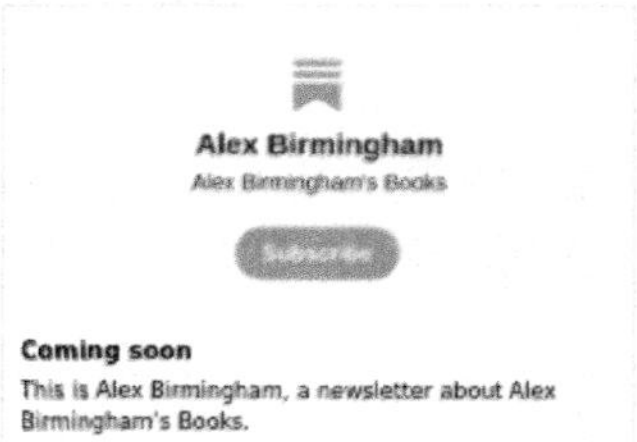

Alex Birmingham Books

Puzzles

Love's Dilemma: Would You Rather? 100 Puzzles for Couples
https://amzn.to/47KTwf5

Holly Jolly Dilemmas: 100 Would You Rather Puzzles
https://amzn.to/3T4g7yK

Positive Vibes: An Adult Puzzles Book
https://amzn.to/4a05Byl

MIAMI: The Ultimate Miami Word Search Puzzle Book
https://amzn.to/3uEwXdv

Books

111 Reconciliation Stories: Imagine & Manifest Your Ex Back https://amzn.to/3R4njs7

Rekindling the Flame: Mastering the Art of Second Chances
https://amzn.to/46AizjK

African Animal Secrets: Fun Facts & Fascinating Creatures
https://amzn.to/3N7G7FI

Affirmation Journals and Workbooks

Radiate Confidence: 111 Affirmations for Self-Love and Inner Strength
https://amzn.to/3Rk0Dn7

Adult Coloring Books

111 Mandalas: An Adult Coloring Book For Calm, Relaxation and Stress Relief with Beautiful and Creative Mandala Designs
https://amzn.to/49SdUfX

Circle Coloring Book: An Adult Coloring Book (111 Circle Patterns)
https://amzn.to/47CcLHA

A Cubist Garden: Artistic Shapes & Flowers Coloring Book for All Ages
https://amzn.to/49SnKhP

Banana: An Adult Coloring Book For Calm, Relaxation and Stress Relief with Abstract Banana Designs
https://amzn.to/3uEw04V

UNICORN HOME SWEET HOME: An Adult Coloring Book For Calm, Relaxation and Stress Relief with Unicorns
https://amzn.to/3RlygH2

UNICORN UNDER THE MOONLIGHT: An Adult Coloring Book
https://amzn.to/49Wg2TM

Kids Coloring Books

Mandala Animals from Costa Rica: A Coloring Journey Through the Rainforest
https://amzn.to/47DhbOG

Mandala Animals from Africa: Coloring and Learning Safari for Kids
https://amzn.to/40YGMyY

The Magical World of Paula the Pony: Coloring Book for Kids
https://amzn.to/4a24KNZ

Toby the Thoughtful Turtle: Coloring Storybook for Kids
https://amzn.to/46HFPfr

111 ZOMBIE GIRLS: A Teen Coloring Book For Calm, Relaxation and Stress Relief with Anime
https://amzn.to/47SRSrj

Robots Coloring Book: Children's Introduction to Robots, Science, Tech, Engineering and Art Through Creativity and Coloring
https://amzn.to/3T4rLcX

Little Toddlers First Big Coloring Book of Alphabets
https://amzn.to/3T34zfe

Little Toddlers First Big Coloring Book of Numbers
https://amzn.to/3QZa63S

Password Logs

C.U.P.S. Crypto Usernames, Passwords and Secrets
https://amzn.to/47RsHWg

Cryptocurrency Wallet Seed Phrase Log Book
https://amzn.to/47VDY84

Daily Planners

Daily Planner: Sunflowers by Vincent Van Gogh
https://amzn.to/3GkwcZF

Daily Planner: Butterfly and Moth Large Daily Planner
https://amzn.to/3sSRHO5

Daily Planner: Neon Snake Animal Print Daily Planner
https://amzn.to/40ZdD6O

Composition Notebooks

Composition Book: Cute Kawaii Cat and Strawberry Notebook
https://amzn.to/47XUfcH

Composition Book: Space, Galaxy and Nebula Notebook
https://amzn.to/3QXU36h

Composition Book: Strawberry Composition Notebook
https://amzn.to/3uFcTrq

Graph Paper Composition Notebook: Black and White Computer Graphic Grid Paper Notebook
https://amzn.to/3GkGPM3

Graph Paper Composition Notebook: Fractal Grid Paper Notebook
https://amzn.to/3GnNuVS

Graph Paper Composition Notebook: Geometric Computer Graphics Grid Paper Notebook
https://amzn.to/3T75NGb

Printed in Great Britain
by Amazon

40013666R00116